THE GHOST BOOK

By William Jaspersohn

Illustrated by Anthony Accardo

Franklin Watts / New York / London / Toronto / Sydney / 1989

Library of Congress Cataloging-in-Publication Data

Jaspersohn, William.
The ghost book / William Jaspersohn; illustrations by Anthony
Accardo.
p.   cm.
Summary: A basic introduction to psychical elements from the Greek
oracles to modern-day poltergeists, including mediums, seances, and
other strange phenomena.
ISBN 0-531-10678-0
1. Ghosts—Juvenile literature. 2. Poltergeists—Juvenile
literature. 3. Spiritualism—Juvenile literature.
[1. Supernatural.] I. Accardo, Anthony, ill. II. Title.
BF1461.J37 1989
133.1—dc19   88-39140   CIP   AC

THE GHOST BOOK

Halloween comes,
and some of us dress up
as ghosts.
But are ghosts real?
What is a ghost, anyway?
And if ghosts are real,
where do they come from?

Some people think that,
besides having a mind and body,
we all have something inside us
called a *spirit*.
They say the spirit gives a body energy
and strength.
They say the spirit
is like the breath of life.
In fact, the word *spirit*
comes from the Latin word *spirare*,
which means "to breathe."

Some people think
that when a person dies,
the spirit lives on and leaves the body.
A ghost, they say,
is the spirit of a dead person
that visits the living.

Some ghosts, these people say, are friendly.
Others are not friendly,
but not really harmful, either.

From the very beginning
of human life,
people all over the world
have believed in ghosts.
Early Stone Age people believed
that if they buried their dead,
the ghosts of the dead people
would not harm them.

The ancient Greeks left honey
and other food for ghosts
near graves.
Wise Greeks, called *oracles*,
could talk to ghosts.
Greeks believed that ghosts
could tell the future.

The ancient Romans believed
that fields and homes
were protected by helpful spirits called
lares.
They also believed that their homes
could be disturbed by mischievous ghosts
called *lemures*.

Throughout history,
these and other peoples—from Indians
to Asians to Europeans—
thought that ghosts and spirits were real.
They were careful
if they thought ghosts
were around them.
Sometimes they were afraid of them.
They wore charms and bracelets
to protect themselves from them.
They tried to treat ghosts well.

Even today,
there are places in the world
where belief in ghosts
is part of everyday life.

In Burma, ghosts seven feet tall,
with long tongues and huge ears and teeth,
are said to live outside villages.
Many Burmese think
these ghosts can cause illness
or even death.
They tell their children, "Watch out!
Shout 'Phyi! phyi!' and spit
when you enter a village.
That will stop ghosts
that might be following you."

Certain tribes in Africa
tell *their* children to watch out, too.
The ghosts are in the gardens
at noon, they say.
The ghosts like to play in the trees.
"You can't go out then,"
mothers tell their children.
"A ghost might hurt you while you play."

Other people believe in different ghosts,
depending on where they live.
Wicked ghosts in the West Indies,
known as *duppies*,
can change into green lizards
and other animals.
Angry ghosts in Japan, called *onryō*,
may haunt the bodies of living people
who have not shown proper respect.

West African ghosts of the Batammaba tribe
dwell by invitation on the ground floor
of family homes.
Nice ghosts and wicked ghosts
are as much a part
of these people's lives
as eating and playing and sleeping.

In America and Europe,
some people believe in ghosts,
and others don't.
But every year there are new reports
of ghost sightings.
And groups like The Ghost Club,
the Society for Psychical Research,
(Suh-sy-uh-tee for sy-ki-kul Re-serch)
both in London, England,
and the American Society for Psychical Research
study the reports
and try to find out
if the "ghosts" that were seen
were really real.

A person who studies a subject
carefully is called a *researcher*.
From their studies,
ghost researchers have concluded
that ghosts appear
in one of two ways:
as ghosts known as *poltergeists*
(POL-ter-guyst),
or
as ghosts known as *haunts*.

Poltergeist comes from a German word
that means "noisy spirit."
Poltergeists are not usually seen,
but they are heard and felt!
People say that poltergeists make
strange rapping noises in houses.
They say they break dishes,
open doors, move furniture,
knock items off shelves,
and generally make mischief
of one kind
or another.

For example,
in a warehouse in Miami, Florida,
some people said that
glasses, ashtrays, and other items
flew off the shelves
and smashed to the floor
all by themselves!
In a house in Olive Hill, Kentucky,
lamps rose off tables
and fell to the floor,
tables spun
and flipped upside down,
cabinets crashed to the floor
again and again.

Nobody knows for sure if
such poltergeist activities really happen.
But researchers have developed
different ideas, or *theories*.
They have noticed
that most poltergeist activity takes place
where there is a young person,
usually a teenager.
There was a young person in the warehouse
in Miami.
There was a young person in the house
in Olive Hill.
Researchers call such a young person
a *focus*, or *focal agent*.
Often, say researchers,
the young person is sad, or angry, or upset.

A poltergeist,
they have concluded,
might be some kind of force, or power,
that comes from the young person
and is caused by his or her anger.
Or it might be a real spirit or ghost
attracted to the unhappy young person.

Whatever poltergeists are, the good
news is that poltergeist activity
rarely lasts very long.
And after a while it finally stops.

*H*aunts, say researchers,
are ghosts that appear
in a certain house or a place outdoors.
Often they appear
where something awful has happened,
such as a murder or a violent death.
In Essex, England, for example,
the ghost of a nun
murdered in the fifteenth century
is said to haunt Borley Rectory.
Sometimes such ghosts are seen.
Other times there is only a creepy feeling
that the haunted location gives off.

Sometimes the ghost appears to keep
doing the same thing over and over,
such as walking back and forth
in the same spot.
Other times the ghost seems free
to move anywhere it wants and
react to other people.

It is said that dogs and cats are able
to see ghosts—
much to their owners' surprise!
Houses have been haunted by
animal ghosts—dogs and cats and horses.

Famous dead people have shown up
as haunts, too.
The ghost of England's Queen Elizabeth I
has been seen in the library
of Windsor Castle.
The ghost of President Abraham Lincoln
has been seen walking in the White House.

What does the average ghost look like?
Usually, say people who have seen them,
a ghost appears pale and wispy,
but some look like we do.
Most are dressed in the clothes they wore
while they were alive.

Often the temperature seems to drop
when a ghost is present.
If the ghost is felt,
it is icy to the touch.

Haunts can be noisy, like poltergeists,
though they don't usually throw
or break things.
Ghosts have been reported
walking on stairs, turning on light switches,
banging on walls, talking in the night.
A ghost in Canada has been heard
playing the piano. But every time
someone tries to catch him at it,
he stops!

What's going on when people see ghosts?
What's going on when they hear them?
Again, nobody knows for sure
what a ghost is.
But, again, researchers have different
theories.

One theory is that people who see or hear
ghosts are *hallucinating*.
That means that their mind is playing
tricks on them. They're just
seeing and hearing things.

Another theory of why there are ghosts
is called the *tape-recording theory*.
This theory states that an awful event,
such as a death-causing accident
or a murder,
leaves some kind of ghostly mark, or
imprint, at the place where the tragedy
occurred. Researchers liken
this imprint to a recording
that plays in thin air!
Somehow, the imprint
stays in that one place.
It might play a picture of the dead person
over and over, or it might play a creepy
feeling, sound, or smell.
It's just a theory, but it might
explain why some ghosts appear to do
the same thing over and over.

The third theory
of why there are ghosts
might be called the *spirit theory*.
The spirit theory says that spirits
are real.
It says that ghosts are really spirits.
People who believe in the spirit theory
of ghosts are called *spiritualists*.

Spiritualists called *mediums* say they can
communicate with ghosts and spirits.
Some mediums hold meetings called *seances*.
There, they speak to spirits
that usually remain invisible.
The spirits answer questions by
knocking on a table—
one knock for "yes," two knocks
for "no."

Other mediums talk to spirits
by means of something called
automatic writing.
The medium holds a pen in his
or her writing hand.
The spirit is said to guide the pen across a page
and write messages.

Still other mediums talk to spirits
by going into a kind of sleep
called a *trance*.
The spirits are said to enter the medium's body
and talk, using the medium's voice.
If someone has a question for the spirit—
about the future, or a problem, or a dead
relative, or a friend—
the spirit answers.
Sometimes people who pose questions
to mediums
are surprised by what the spirits
already know about them.

Of course, many people believe
that ghosts, poltergeists, and mediums
are fakes.
Someone says a house is haunted,
or says he can talk to spirits,
to get attention or make money or
become famous.
Once, for example, a house in England
was said to be disturbed by a poltergeist.
It seemed to be responsible
for mysteriously moving a plant
from one room to another.
A man who studied ghosts
came to investigate.
He discovered that a girl in the house
was the one moving the plant
when no one was looking.
There was no poltergeist.
The girl had been playing a sneaky trick,
one that upset a lot of people.

So what are we to think?
What should our feelings be?
What should we think about ghosts?
About one in ten people
believe they have seen
or heard them,
but nobody knows for sure
if ghosts are real or not.
They might be,
but no one can explain why.
Perhaps the best thing to do
is keep an open mind.
That way we're always ready for answers.

P.S. If you ever happen
to see a ghost,
don't be afraid.
Ghosts in real life harm nobody.
Just give him or her a big hello,
and wish the ghost a very nice day.

GLOSSARY

Automatic writing—writing done without plan or design, and sometimes without awareness, as if guided by an outside agent, such as a ghost or spirit.

Duppy—a wicked ghost of the West Indies.

Focus, or focal agent—a person, usually young, believed to be the reason or cause for a given poltergeist activity.

Hallucinating—having visions or imaginary perceptions; "seeing things" that are not real.

Haunt—a ghost that appears in a particular place, either indoors or outdoors.

Lar—a ghost or spirit of the ancient Romans, believed to protect houses, fields, crops, etc.

Lemures—mischievous ghosts of ancient Rome.

Medium—any spiritualist who claims to be able to communicate with ghosts or spirits.

Onryō—an angry ghost of the Japanese, believed to be able to haunt the bodies of living people who have not shown proper respect.

Oracle—a medium of the ancient Greeks and other ancient peoples said to be able to communicate with pagan gods, ghosts, and spirits.

Poltergeist—a German word, literally meaning "knocking, rattling, or noisy spirit."

Seance—a meeting, conducted by a medium, with the ghost or spirit of a dead person.

Spirit—from the Latin word, *spirare*, meaning "to breathe." Believed by some to be the source of life and energy for any living body; also believed by some to live on and leave a body that dies.

Spirit theory—a theory about the existence of ghosts and spirits that says that ghosts and spirits are real.

Spiritualist—one who believes in the existence of spirits and ghosts.

Tape-recording theory—a theory, about why some ghosts and spirits appear to do the same thing repeatedly, that states that an awful event, such as a tragic accident or murder, leaves a kind of ghostly mark or imprint capable of playing over and over, like a recording.